coffee morning cakes

Essential dishes for everyday cooking

Love Food ® is an imprint of Parragon Books Ltd

Parragon
Queen Street House
4 Queen Street
Bath BA1 1HE, UK

ISBN: 978-1-4075-2870-0

Printed in Indonesia

Designed by Talking Design
Cover text and introduction by Lorraine Turner

Notes for the reader
This book uses both metric and imperial measurements. Follow the same units of measurement throughout; do not mix metric with imperial. All spoon measurements are level, unless otherwise stated: teaspoons are assumed to be 5ml and tablespoons are assumed to be 15ml. Unless otherwise stated, milk is assumed to be semi-skimmed, eggs and individual vegetables such as potatoes are medium, and pepper is freshly ground black pepper. Recipes using raw or very lightly cooked eggs should be avoided by infants, the elderly, pregnant women, convalescents and anyone suffering from an illness. The times given are an approximate guide only.

Contents

Introduction 4

Classic Cakes 6

A Little Something 26

Cookies, Bars & Buns 44

Pure Indulgence 62

Index 80

introduction

Coffee has experienced a revival these days, and the multitude of coffee shops springing up in every shopping centre is a testimony to its increasing popularity. Along with this renewed thirst has come the rebirth of its much-loved partner: cake. What could be better than nibbling on a mouthwatering piece of sticky chocolate brownie while sipping a cup of delicious cappuccino?

For informal entertaining, nothing can beat the taste and smell of a fresh brew and lovingly prepared sweet treats. Coffee and cakes are also the perfect way to round off a dinner party. When you're not entertaining, why not snatch a few moments to yourself, put your feet up and treat yourself to a cup of hot steaming mocha and some irresistible Victoria sandwich?

Coffee, and various teas, have a strong flavour, so the cakes or accompanying sweets that you choose must have a sufficiently strong flavour of their own in order not to be overwhelmed. Chocolate is the perfect partner for coffee: it creates a rich, dark taste explosion that will tantalize your taste buds and those of your guests. Cakes containing different kinds of nuts, such as walnuts, pecan nuts and almonds, are also ideal. The flavour of coconut goes well with coffee, and don't forget that most luxurious partner of all – cream – a combination made in heaven!

Preparing and cooking cakes

Making wonderful cakes and bakes is easy – if you have children, they will enjoy helping you to bake them too, making even lighter work! Simply give them an apron and a wooden spoon and they can help you mix the ingredients. They will also have fun decorating the cakes with hundreds and thousands, glacé cherries, chocolate chips, coloured icing, marshmallows, coffee beans, sweets and whatever else appeals to the imagination. Just remember to allow a little more time for cleaning up afterwards!

Here are a few simple tips to help you create successful cakes every time:

- Do not store your flour for too long, especially self-raising flour, or you could end up with a sunken cake.

- About 30 minutes before you start, bring all of the ingredients to room temperature to make beating and whisking easier.

- Preheat the oven while you are preparing the mixture, so that the oven is sufficiently hot before you put in the cake mixture. This will help your cake mixture to rise quickly and easily.

- Sift your flour twice to incorporate more air and thus create a lighter cake.

- Follow the recipe instructions exactly. For example, some instructions are designed to enable more air to get into the mixture and ensure a lighter cake.

- Avoid opening the oven door until the last few minutes of the cooking time or your cake will sink.

- When using chocolate, opt for bars that contain at least 70% cocoa solids.

- Remember that oven temperatures and cooking times vary, so you may need to make more than one batch of cakes to get used to how your oven functions. Make any necessary adjustments, note any changes on your favourite recipes, and keep for future reference.

Essential equipment

You don't need lots of special equipment to prepare and bake exciting cakes – just a few basic items will get you started.

At least one large mixing bowl is essential. You will also need a selection of cake tins: a springform tin is ideal for large cakes, and you will find a couple of 12-hole muffin tins very helpful for making smaller cakes. You will also need a couple of sandwich tins for baking two-tier sponge cakes. You can add other tins, such as a Swiss roll tin, as your time and budget allow.

Other items you will need include a set of kitchen scales and a measuring jug for weighing/ measuring ingredients, a sieve, a whisk, a grater, a wooden spoon and a spatula. A food mixer will save you a lot of time when preparing the cake mixture, but is not essential.

classic **cakes**

Victoria *Sandwich Cake*

SERVES 8

175 g/6 oz butter, softened
175 g/6 oz caster sugar
3 eggs, beaten
175 g/6 oz self-raising flour
pinch of salt
3 tbsp raspberry jam
1 tbsp caster or icing sugar

Preheat the oven to 180°C/350°F/Gas Mark 4. Grease two 20-cm/8-inch sponge tins and line the bases with greaseproof paper or baking paper.

Cream the butter and sugar together in a mixing bowl, using a wooden spoon or a hand-held mixer, until the mixture is pale in colour and light and fluffy. Add the egg a little at a time, beating well after each addition. Sift the flour and salt and carefully add to the mixture, folding it in with a metal spoon or a spatula.

Divide the mixture between the tins and smooth over with the spatula. Place them on the same shelf in the centre of the oven and bake for 25–30 minutes, until well risen, golden brown and beginning to shrink from the sides of the tin.

Remove from the oven and allow to stand for 1 minute. Loosen the cakes from around the edge of the tins using a palette knife. Turn the cakes out onto a clean tea towel, remove the paper and invert them onto a wire rack. When completely cool, sandwich together with the jam and sprinkle with the sugar. This cake is delicious when freshly baked, but any remaining cake can be stored in an airtight tin for up to 1 week.

Chocolate
Fudge Cake

SERVES 8

- 175 g/6 oz unsalted butter, softened, plus extra for greasing
- 175 g/6 oz golden caster sugar
- 3 eggs, beaten
- 3 tbsp golden syrup
- 40 g/1½ oz ground almonds
- 175 g/6 oz self-raising flour
- pinch of salt
- 40 g/1½ oz cocoa powder

Icing

- 225 g/8 oz plain chocolate, broken into pieces
- 55 g/2 oz dark muscovado sugar
- 225 g/8 oz unsalted butter, diced
- 5 tbsp evaporated milk
- ½ tsp vanilla extract

Grease and line the bases of two 20-cm/8-inch cake tins. To make the icing, place the chocolate, sugar, butter, evaporated milk and vanilla extract in a heavy-based saucepan. Heat gently, stirring constantly, until melted. Pour into a bowl and leave to cool. Cover and chill in the refrigerator, or until spreadable.

Preheat the oven to 180°C/350°F/Gas Mark 4. Place the butter and sugar in a bowl and beat together until light and fluffy. Gradually beat in the eggs. Stir in the golden syrup and ground almonds. Sift the flour, salt and cocoa powder into a separate bowl, then fold into the mixture. Add a little water, if necessary, to make a dropping consistency. Spoon the mixture into the prepared tins and bake in the oven for 30–35 minutes, or until springy to the touch and a skewer inserted in the centre comes out clean.

Leave the cakes in the tins for 5 minutes, then turn out on to wire racks to cool completely. When the cakes are cold, sandwich them together with half the icing. Spread the remaining icing over the top and sides of the cake, swirling it to give a frosted appearance.

Carrot
Cake

SERVES 8

butter, for greasing
175 g/6 oz light muscovado sugar
3 eggs
175 ml/6 fl oz sunflower oil
175 g/6 oz coarsely grated carrot
2 ripe bananas, mashed
55 g/2 oz walnuts, chopped
280 g/10 oz plain flour
½ tsp salt
1 tsp bicarbonate of soda
2 tsp baking powder

Frosting

200 g/7 oz cream cheese
½ tsp vanilla extract
115 g/4 oz icing sugar
25 g/1 oz walnuts, chopped

Preheat the oven to 180°C/350°F/Gas Mark 4. Grease and line the base of a 23-cm/9-inch springform cake tin. Place the sugar, eggs, sunflower oil, carrots, bananas and walnuts in a bowl. Sift in the flour, salt, bicarbonate of soda and baking powder. Beat the mixture until smooth.

Turn the mixture into the prepared tin and bake in the preheated oven for about 1 hour, or until well risen and golden brown and a skewer inserted into the centre comes out clean. Leave in the tin for 10 minutes, then turn out and peel off the lining paper. Transfer to a wire rack to cool completely.

To make the frosting, place the cream cheese and vanilla extract in a bowl and beat well to soften. Beat in the icing sugar, a tablespoon at a time, until smooth. Swirl over the cake and sprinkle the chopped walnuts on top. Leave in a cool place for the frosting to harden slightly before serving.

Apple
Cake

SERVES 12

225 g/8 oz unsalted butter, diced, plus extra for greasing
3 apples, peeled, cored and sliced
100 g/3½ oz unrefined caster sugar
100 g/3½ oz demerara sugar
½ tsp vanilla extract
½ tsp ground cinnamon
4 large eggs
100 g/3½ oz wholemeal self-raising flour
125 g/4½ oz white self-raising flour
1 tsp baking powder
1 tbsp clear honey
3–4 slices dried apple, chopped

Preheat the oven to 180°C/350°F/Gas Mark 4. Grease and line a 23-cm/9-inch round cake tin. Arrange the apple slices in the bottom of the prepared tin.

Put all the remaining ingredients, except the honey and dried apple, in a food processor and pulse until well combined. Pour the cake mixture over the apples and bake in the preheated oven for 1 hour until cooked through – a skewer inserted into the centre of the cake should come out clean.

Remove from the oven and leave to cool in the tin, then invert onto a plate and remove the lining paper. Turn back over onto a serving plate. Spread the top of the cake with the honey and scatter over the dried apple. Cut into 12 equal pieces.

Battenberg
Cake

SERVES 8

1 x Victoria Sandwich mixture (see page 8) flavoured and coloured with vanilla; orange and chocolate; or lemon and orange
2–3 tbsp apricot jam
300 g/10 oz marzipan, flavoured with 3 tbsp sifted cocoa powder for the orange chocolate cake
caster sugar
pink and green edible food colouring if making the vanilla cake

Preheat the oven to 180°C/350°F/Gas Mark 4. Grease and line an 18-cm/7-inch shallow, square baking tin. Cut a strip of double greaseproof paper and grease it. Use this to divide the tin in half.

Prepare the sponge mixture, flavour it with vanilla, if liked, and divide in half. Colour the vanilla portions pink and green. Alternatively, instead of vanilla, use chocolate in one portion and orange in the other, or lemon in one portion and orange in the other. Colour the orange portion with a little orange food colouring. Spoon one mixture into half the prepared baking tin, keeping the paper in the middle, and spoon the other into the other half. Try to make the divide as straight as possible. Bake in the middle of the oven for 35–40 minutes. Turn out and cool on a wire rack.

When cool, trim the edges and cut the cake portions lengthways in half, making four equal parts. Warm the jam in a small saucepan. Brush two sides of each portion of cake with jam and stick them together to give a chequerboard effect. Roll out the marzipan to a rectangle wide and long enough to wrap around the cake. Trim the edges neatly. Brush the outside of the cake with jam. Place the cake on the marzipan and wrap the paste around the cake. Dampen the edges lightly to form a neat join at one of the corners of the cake.

Pinch the top and bottom edges of the paste into a pattern with crimpers. Serve immediately.

Coffee
Streusel Cake

SERVES 8

100 g/3½ oz butter, melted and cooled, plus extra for greasing
275 g/9½ oz plain flour
1 tbsp baking powder
75 g/2¾ oz caster sugar
150 ml/5 fl oz milk
2 eggs
2 tbsp instant coffee mixed with 1 tbsp boiling water
50 g/1¾ oz almonds, chopped
icing sugar, for dusting

Topping

75 g/2¾ oz self-raising flour
75 g/2¾ oz demerara sugar
2 tbsp butter, diced
1 tsp ground mixed spice
1 tbsp water

Preheat the oven to 190°C/375°F/Gas Mark 5. Grease a 23-cm/9-inch loose-based round cake tin with butter and line with baking paper. Sift the flour and baking powder together into a large mixing bowl, then stir in the caster sugar.

Whisk the milk, eggs, melted butter and coffee mixture together and pour onto the dry ingredients. Add the chopped almonds and mix lightly together. Spoon the mixture into the prepared tin.

To make the topping, mix the flour and sugar together. Rub in the butter with your fingertips until the mixture resembles breadcrumbs. Sprinkle in the mixed spice and water and bring the mixture together into loose crumbs. Sprinkle the topping evenly over the surface of the cake mixture in the tin.

Bake in the preheated oven for about 1 hour. If the topping starts to brown too quickly, cover loosely with foil. Leave to cool in the tin. Turn out, dust with icing sugar and serve.

Lemon
Drizzle Cake

SERVES 8

butter, for greasing
200 g/7 oz plain flour
2 tsp baking powder
200 g/7 oz caster sugar
4 eggs
150 ml/5 fl oz soured cream
grated rind of 1 large lemon
4 tbsp lemon juice
150 ml/5 fl oz sunflower oil

Syrup

4 tbsp icing sugar
3 tbsp lemon juice

Preheat the oven to 180°C/350°F/Gas Mark 4. Lightly grease a 20-cm/8-inch loose-based round cake tin and line the base with baking paper.

Sift the flour and baking powder into a mixing bowl and stir in the caster sugar. In a separate bowl, whisk the eggs, soured cream, lemon rind, lemon juice and oil together.

Pour the egg mixture into the dry ingredients and mix well until evenly combined.

Pour the mixture into the prepared tin and bake in the preheated oven for 45–60 minutes, until risen and golden brown.

Meanwhile, to make the syrup, mix together the icing sugar and lemon juice in a small saucepan. Stir over a low heat until just beginning to bubble and turn syrupy.

As soon as the cake comes out of the oven, prick the surface with a fine skewer, then brush the syrup over the top. Leave the cake to cool completely in the tin before turning out and serving.

Almond & Hazelnut
Gateau

SERVES 8

butter, for greasing
4 eggs
100 g/3½ oz caster sugar
50 g/1¾ oz ground almonds
50 g/1¾ oz ground hazelnuts
5½ tbsp plain flour
50 g/1¾ oz flaked almonds
icing sugar, for dusting

Filling

100 g/3½ oz plain chocolate
1 tbsp butter
300 ml/10 fl oz double cream

Preheat the oven to 190°C/375°F/Gas Mark 5. Grease and line the bases of two 18-cm/7-inch round sandwich tins.

Whisk the eggs and caster sugar together for 10 minutes, or until very light and foamy and the whisk leaves a trail that lasts a few seconds when lifted. Fold in the ground almonds and hazelnuts, sift the flour and fold in with a metal spoon or spatula. Pour into the prepared tins.

Sprinkle the flaked almonds over the top of one of the cakes, then bake both cakes in the preheated oven for 15–20 minutes, or until springy to the touch. Leave to cool in the tins for 5 minutes, then turn out onto wire racks to cool completely.

To make the filling, melt the chocolate, remove from the heat and stir in the butter. Leave to cool. Whip the cream until it holds its shape, then fold in the chocolate until mixed.

Place the cake without the extra almonds on a serving plate and spread the filling over it. Leave to set slightly, then place the almond-topped cake on top of the filling and leave to chill in the refrigerator for 1 hour. Dust with icing sugar and serve.

Clementine Cake

SERVES 8

175 g/6 oz butter, softened, plus extra for greasing
2 clementines
175 g/6 oz caster sugar
3 eggs, lightly beaten
175 g/6 oz self-raising flour
3 tbsp ground almonds
3 tbsp single cream

Glaze & Topping

6 tbsp clementine juice
2 tbsp caster sugar
3 white sugar lumps, crushed

Preheat the oven to 180°C/350°F/Gas Mark 4. Grease an 18-cm/7-inch round cake tin and line the base with baking paper.

Pare the rind from the clementines and finely chop. Cream the butter, sugar and clementine rind together in a bowl until pale and fluffy.

Add the eggs, a little at a time, beating well after each addition. Gently fold in the flour, ground almonds and cream. Spoon the mixture into the prepared tin.

Bake in the preheated oven for about 1 hour, or until a fine skewer inserted into the centre comes out clean. Leave to cool slightly.

Meanwhile, to make the glaze, put the clementine juice in a small saucepan with the caster sugar over a medium–low heat. Bring to the boil, then reduce the heat and simmer for 5 minutes.

Turn out the cake onto a wire rack. Drizzle the glaze over the cake until it has been absorbed and sprinkle with the crushed sugar lumps.

Leave to cool completely before serving.

a little **something**

Drizzled
Honey Cupcakes

MAKES 12

85 g/3 oz self-raising flour
¼ tsp ground cinnamon
pinch of ground cloves
pinch of grated nutmeg
85 g/3 oz butter, softened
85 g/3 oz caster sugar
1 tbsp runny honey
finely grated rind of 1 orange
2 eggs, lightly beaten
40 g/1½ oz walnut pieces, finely chopped

Topping

15 g/½ oz walnut pieces, finely chopped
½ tsp ground cinnamon
2 tbsp runny honey
juice of 1 orange

Preheat the oven to 190°C/375°F/Gas Mark 5. Put 12 paper baking cases in a muffin tin, or put 12 double-layer paper cases on a baking tray.

Sift the flour, cinnamon, cloves and nutmeg together into a bowl. Put the butter and sugar in a separate bowl and beat together until light and fluffy. Beat in the honey and orange rind, then gradually add the eggs, beating well after each addition. Using a metal spoon, fold in the flour mixture. Stir in the walnuts, then spoon the mixture into the paper cases.

Bake the cupcakes in the preheated oven for 20 minutes, or until well risen and golden brown. Transfer to a wire rack and leave to cool.

To make the topping, mix together the walnuts and cinnamon. Put the honey and orange juice in a saucepan and heat gently, stirring, until combined.

When the cupcakes have almost cooled, prick the tops all over with a fork or skewer and then drizzle with the warm honey mixture. Sprinkle the walnut mixture over the top of each cupcake and serve warm or cold.

Moist
Walnut Cupcakes

MAKES 12

85 g/3 oz walnuts
55 g/2 oz butter, softened
100 g/3½ oz caster sugar
grated rind of ½ lemon
70 g/2½ oz self-raising flour
2 eggs
12 walnut halves, to decorate

Icing

55 g/2 oz butter, softened
85 g/3 oz icing sugar
grated rind of ½ lemon
1 tsp lemon juice

Preheat the oven to 190°C/375°F/Gas Mark 5. Put 12 paper baking cases in a muffin tin, or put 12 double-layer paper cases on a baking tray.

Put the walnuts in a food processor and pulse, until finely ground, being careful not to over-grind, which will turn them to oil. Add the butter, cut into small pieces, along with the sugar, lemon rind, flour and eggs, then blend until evenly mixed. Spoon the mixture into the paper cases.

Bake the cupcakes in the preheated oven for 20 minutes, or until well risen and golden brown. Transfer to a wire rack and leave to cool.

To make the icing, put the butter in a bowl and beat until fluffy. Sift in the icing sugar, add the lemon rind and juice and mix well together.

When the cupcakes are cold, spread the icing on top of each cupcake and top with a walnut half to decorate.

Lemon Butterfly
Cakes

MAKES 12

115 g/4 oz self-raising flour
½ tsp baking powder
115 g/4 oz soft tub margarine
115 g/4 oz caster sugar
2 eggs, lightly beaten
finely grated rind of ½ lemon
2 tbsp milk
icing sugar, for dusting

Lemon Filling

85 g/3 oz butter, softened
175/6 oz icing sugar
1 tbsp lemon juice

Preheat the oven to 190°C/375°F/Gas Mark 5. Put 12 paper baking cases in a muffin tin, or put 12 double-layer paper cases on a baking tray.

Sift the flour and baking powder into a large bowl. Add the margarine, sugar, eggs, lemon rind and milk and, using a wooden spoon or a hand-held mixer, beat together until smooth. Spoon the mixture into the paper cases.

Bake the cupcakes in the preheated oven for 15–20 minutes, or until well risen and golden brown. Transfer to a wire rack and leave to cool.

To make the filling, put the butter in a bowl and beat until fluffy. Sift in the icing sugar, add the lemon juice and beat together until smooth and creamy.

When the cupcakes are cold, use a serrated knife to cut a circle from the top of each cupcake and then cut each circle in half. Spread or pipe a little of the lemon filling into the centre of each cupcake, then press 2 semi-circular halves into it at an angle to resemble butterfly wings. Dust with sifted icing sugar before serving.

Mochachino Brownies
with White Mocha Sauce

MAKES 8–9

115 g/4 oz unsalted butter, plus extra for greasing
115 g/4 oz plain chocolate
2 tbsp strong black coffee
250 g/9 oz golden caster sugar
½ tsp ground cinnamon
3 eggs, beaten
85 g/3 oz plain flour
55 g/2 oz milk chocolate chips
55 g/2 oz toasted walnuts, skinned and chopped, plus extra to decorate

White Mocha Sauce

100 ml/3½ fl oz double cream
85 g/3 oz white chocolate
1 tbsp strong black coffee

Preheat the oven to 180°C/350°F/Gas Mark 4. Grease and line a 23-cm/9-inch square baking tin.

Place the butter, chocolate and coffee in a medium-sized saucepan over a low heat and stir until just melted and smooth. Cool slightly.

Whisk in the sugar, cinnamon and eggs. Beat in the flour, chocolate chips and walnuts. Pour the mixture into the prepared tin.

Bake in the oven for 30–35 minutes, until just firm but still moist inside. Cool in the tin then cut into squares or bars.

Meanwhile, make the sauce by placing all the ingredients in a small saucepan over a low heat, stirring occasionally, until melted and smooth.

Place the brownies on individual plates and spoon the warm sauce on top. Decorate with chopped walnuts and serve.

Sticky Chocolate
Brownies

MAKES 9

85 g/3 oz butter, unsalted for preference, plus extra for greasing
140 g/5 oz caster sugar
100 g/3½ oz soft brown sugar
125 g/4½ oz plain chocolate
1 tbsp golden syrup
2 eggs
1 tsp chocolate extract or vanilla extract
100 g/3½ oz plain flour
2 tbsp cocoa powder, plus extra for dusting
½ tsp baking powder

Preheat the oven to 180°C/350°F/Gas Mark 4. Lightly grease a 20-cm/8-inch square baking tin and line the base.

Place the butter, caster sugar, soft brown sugar, chocolate and golden syrup in a heavy-based saucepan and heat gently, stirring until the mixture is well blended and smooth. Remove from the heat and leave to cool.

Beat the eggs and chocolate extract together. Whisk in the cooled chocolate mixture. Sift the flour, cocoa and baking powder together and fold carefully into the egg and chocolate mixture using a metal spoon or palette knife.

Spoon the mixture into the prepared tin and bake in the preheated oven for 25 minutes, until the top is crisp and the edge of the cake is starting to shrink away from the tin. The inside of the cake will still be quite gooey and soft to the touch.

Leave to cool completely in the tin, dust with cocoa powder, then cut into squares and serve.

Upside-Down Toffee Apple Brownies

MAKES 9

115 g/4 oz unsalted butter, plus extra for greasing
175 g/6 oz light muscovado sugar
2 eggs, beaten
200 g/7 oz plain flour
1 tsp baking powder
½ tsp bicarbonate of soda
1½ tsp ground mixed spice
2 eating apples, peeled and coarsely grated
85 g/3 oz hazelnuts, chopped

Toffee Apple Topping

85 g/3 oz light muscovado sugar
55 g/2 oz unsalted butter
1 dessert apple, cored and thinly sliced

Preheat the oven to 180°C/350°F/Gas Mark 4. Grease a 23-cm/9-inch square shallow baking tin.

To make the topping, place the muscovado sugar and butter in a small saucepan and heat gently, stirring, until melted. Pour into the prepared tin. Arrange the apple slices over the mixture.

To make the brownies, place the butter and sugar in a bowl and beat well until pale and fluffy. Beat in the eggs gradually.

Sift together the flour, baking powder, bicarbonate of soda and mixed spice, and fold into the mixture. Stir in the apples and nuts.

Pour into the prepared tin and bake for 35–40 minutes, until firm and golden. Leave to cool in the tin for 10 minutes, then turn out and cut into squares.

Pecan
Brownies

MAKES 20

225 g/8 oz unsalted butter, plus extra for greasing
70 g/2½ oz plain chocolate
125 g/4½ oz plain flour
3/4 tsp bicarbonate of soda
1/4 tsp baking powder
55 g/2 oz pecan nuts
100 g/3½ oz demerara sugar, plus extra for decorating
½ tsp almond extract
1 egg
1 tsp milk

Preheat the oven to 180°C/350°F/Gas Mark 4. Grease and line a 28 x 18-cm/11 x 7-inch rectangular baking tin.

Put the chocolate in a heatproof bowl set over a saucepan of gently simmering water and heat until it is melted. Meanwhile, sift the flour, bicarbonate of soda and baking powder together into a large bowl.

Finely chop the pecan nuts and set aside. In a separate bowl, cream together the butter and sugar, then mix in the almond extract and the egg. Remove the chocolate from the heat and stir into the butter mixture. Add the flour mixture, milk and chopped nuts to the bowl and stir until well combined.

Spoon the mixture into the prepared tin and smooth it. Transfer to the preheated oven and cook for 30 minutes, or until firm to the touch (it should still be a little soft in the centre). Remove from the oven and leave to cool completely. Sprinkle with the sugar, cut into 20 squares and serve.

Cappuccino
Brownies

MAKES 15

- 225 g/8 oz butter, softened, plus extra for greasing
- 225 g/8 oz self-raising flour
- 1 tsp baking powder
- 1 tsp cocoa powder, plus extra for dusting
- 225 g/8 oz golden caster sugar
- 4 eggs, beaten
- 3 tbsp instant coffee granules, dissolved in 2 tbsp hot water, cooled
- cocoa powder, for dusting

White Chocolate Frosting

- 115 g/4 oz white chocolate, broken into pieces
- 55 g/2 oz butter, softened
- 3 tbsp milk
- 175 g/6 oz icing sugar

Preheat the oven to 180°C/350°F/Gas Mark 4. Grease and line the base of a shallow 28 x 18-cm/11 x 7-inch rectangular baking tin.

Sift the flour, baking powder and cocoa into a bowl and add the butter, sugar, eggs and coffee. Beat well, by hand or with an electric whisk, until smooth, then spoon into the prepared tin and smooth the top.

Bake in the oven for 35–40 minutes, or until risen and firm. Leave to cool in the tin for 10 minutes, then turn out onto a wire rack and peel off the lining paper. Leave to cool completely.

To make the frosting, place the chocolate, butter and milk in a bowl set over a saucepan of simmering water and stir until the chocolate has melted. Remove the bowl from the saucepan and sift in the icing sugar. Beat until smooth, then spread over the cake. Dust the top of the cake with sifted cocoa powder, then cut into squares.

cookies, bars & buns

Chocolate Chip Oaties

MAKES 20

115 g/4 oz unsalted butter, softened, plus extra for greasing
115 g/4 oz light muscovado sugar
1 egg
70 g/2½ oz rolled oats
1 tbsp milk
1 tsp vanilla extract
140 g/5 oz plain flour
1 tbsp cocoa powder
½ tsp baking powder
6 squares plain chocolate, broken into pieces
6 squares milk chocolate, broken into pieces

Preheat the oven to 180°C/350°F/Gas Mark 4. Grease 2 large baking trays. Place the butter and sugar in a bowl and beat together with a wooden spoon until light and fluffy.

Beat in the egg, then add the oats, milk and vanilla extract. Beat together until well blended. Sift the flour, cocoa and baking powder into the mixture and stir. Stir in the chocolate pieces.

Place tablespoonfuls of the mixture on the prepared baking trays and flatten slightly with a fork. Bake in the preheated oven for 15 minutes, or until slightly risen and firm. Remove from the oven and cool on the baking trays for 2 minutes, then transfer to wire racks to cool completely.

Mocha Walnut
Cookies

MAKES ABOUT 16

- 115 g/4 oz unsalted butter, softened, plus extra for greasing
- 115 g/4 oz light muscovado sugar
- 115 g/4 oz golden granulated sugar
- 1 tsp vanilla extract
- 1 tbsp instant coffee granules, dissolved in 1 tbsp hot water
- 1 egg
- 175 g/6 oz plain flour
- ½ tsp baking powder
- ¼ tsp bicarbonate of soda
- 55 g/2 oz milk chocolate chips
- 60 g/2¼ oz shelled walnuts, coarsely chopped

Preheat the oven to 180°C/350°F/Gas Mark 4. Grease 2 large baking trays with a little butter. Place the butter, muscovado sugar and granulated sugar in a large bowl and beat together thoroughly until light and fluffy. Place the vanilla extract, coffee mixture and egg in a separate large bowl and whisk together.

Gradually add the coffee mixture to the butter and sugar, beating until fluffy. Sift the flour, baking powder and bicarbonate of soda into the mixture and fold in carefully. Fold in the chocolate chips and walnuts.

Drop dessertspoonfuls of the mixture onto the prepared baking trays, spacing well apart to allow room for spreading. Bake in the preheated oven for 10–15 minutes, or until crisp on the outside but still soft inside. Remove from the oven. Cool on the baking trays for 2 minutes, then transfer to wire racks to cool completely.

Apricot Oat-Style
Bars

MAKES 10

corn oil, for oiling
175 g/6 oz soft tub margarine
115 g/4 oz demerara sugar
2 tbsp runny honey
55 g/2 oz dried apricots, chopped
2 tsp sesame seeds
150 g/5½ oz rolled oats

Preheat the oven to 180°C/350°F/Gas Mark 4. Very lightly oil a 26 x 17-cm/10½ x 6½-inch shallow cake pan.

Put the spread, sugar and honey into a small saucepan over a low heat and heat until the ingredients have melted together – do not let the mixture boil. When the ingredients are warm and well combined, stir in the apricots, sesame seeds and oats.

Spoon the mixture into the prepared tin and lightly level with the back of a spoon. Cook in the preheated oven for 20–25 minutes, or until golden brown. Remove from the oven, then cut into 10 bars and leave to cool completely before removing from the cake tin. Store the bars in an airtight container and consume within 2–3 days.

Hazelnut
Chocolate Crunch

MAKES 12

115 g/4 oz unsalted butter, plus extra for greasing
200 g/7 oz rolled oats
55 g/2 oz hazelnuts, lightly toasted and chopped
55 g/2 oz plain flour
85 g/3 oz light muscovado sugar
2 tbsp golden syrup
55 g/2 oz plain chocolate chips

Preheat the oven to 180°C/350°F/Gas Mark 4. Grease a 23-cm/9-inch square shallow baking tin.

Mix the oats, hazelnuts and flour in a large bowl. Place the butter, sugar and syrup in a large saucepan and heat gently until the sugar has dissolved. Pour in the dry ingredients and mix well. Stir in the chocolate chips.

Turn the mixture into the prepared tin and bake in the preheated oven for 20–25 minutes, or until golden brown and firm to the touch. Using a knife, mark into 12 triangles and leave to cool in the tin. Cut the hazelnut chocolate crunch triangles with a sharp knife before carefully removing them from the tin.

Fruit & Nut
Squares

MAKES 9

115 g/4 oz unsalted butter, plus extra for greasing
2 tbsp runny honey
1 egg, beaten
150 g/5½ oz ground almonds
115 g/4 oz dried apricots, finely chopped
55 g/2 oz dried cherries
55 g/2 oz toasted hazelnuts
2 tbsp sesame seeds
100 g/3½ oz rolled oats

Preheat the oven to 180°C/350°F/Gas Mark 4. Lightly grease an 18-cm/7-inch shallow square cake tin with butter. Beat the remaining butter with the honey in a bowl until creamy, then beat in the egg with the almonds.

Add the remaining ingredients and mix together well. Press into the tin, ensuring that the mixture is firmly packed. Smooth the top.

Transfer to the preheated oven and bake for 20–25 minutes, or until firm to the touch and golden brown.

Remove from the oven and Leave to stand for 10 minutes before marking into squares. Leave to stand until cold before removing from the tin. Cut into squares, store in an airtight container and consume within 2–3 days.

Rolled Fruit Buns

MAKES 9

2 tbsp butter, diced, plus extra for greasing
225 g/8 oz strong white flour, plus extra for dusting
½ tsp salt
1½ tsp easy-blend dried yeast
1 tsp golden caster sugar
125 ml/4 fl oz lukewarm milk
1 egg, beaten
oil, for oiling
85 g/3 oz icing sugar

Filling

55 g/2 oz light muscovado sugar
115 g/4 oz luxury mixed dried fruit
1 tsp ground mixed spice
4 tbsp butter, softened

Preheat the oven to 190°C/375°F/Gas Mark 5. Grease an 18-cm/7-inch square cake tin. Sift the flour and salt together into a warmed bowl, then stir in the yeast and caster sugar. Rub in the butter with your fingertips until the mixture resembles breadcrumbs. Make a well in the centre. Mix the milk and egg together and add to the well. Mix to form a soft dough. Turn out the dough onto a lightly floured work surface and knead for 5–10 minutes, or until smooth and elastic. Put in an oiled bowl, cover with clingfilm and leave to rise in a warm place for 1 hour, or until doubled in size. Turn out the dough again and knead lightly for 1 minute. Roll out into a rectangle 30 x 23 cm/12 x 9 inches.

To make the filling, mix the muscovado sugar, dried fruit and mixed spice together in a bowl. Spread the dough with the butter and sprinkle the fruit mixture on top. Roll up, starting from one long edge. Cut into 9 slices and arrange, cut-side up, in the prepared tin. Cover with oiled clingfilm and leave to prove in a warm place for 45 minutes.

Bake the buns in the preheated oven for 30 minutes, or until golden. Leave to cool in the tin for 10 minutes, then transfer, in one piece, to a wire rack and leave to cool completely. Sift the icing sugar into a bowl and stir in enough water to make a thin glaze. Brush over the buns and leave to set. Pull the buns apart to serve.

Blueberry Bran *Muffins*

MAKES 10

150 g/5½ oz plain white flour
100 g/3½ oz self-raising wholemeal flour
1 tbsp oat bran
2 tsp baking powder
½ tsp bicarbonate of soda
pinch of salt
50 g/1¾ oz demerara sugar
1 tbsp runny honey
1 large egg
200 ml/7 fl oz buttermilk
150 g/5½ oz fresh blueberries

Preheat the oven to 180°C/350°F/Gas Mark 4. Line 10 holes of a muffin tin with muffin paper cases.

Mix the plain flour, self-raising flour, bran, baking powder, bicarbonate of soda and salt together in a bowl and stir in the sugar. Whisk the honey, egg and buttermilk together in a jug.

Pour the wet ingredients into the dry ingredients and stir briefly to combine. Don't overmix – the mixture should still be a little lumpy. Fold in the blueberries.

Spoon the mixture into the paper cases and bake in the preheated oven for 20 minutes until risen and lightly browned.

Remove the muffins from the oven and leave to cool in the tin. Serve warm or cold.

Chocolate
Eclairs

MAKES 12

Choux Pastry

70 g/2½ oz butter, cut into small pieces, plus extra for greasing
150 ml/5 fl oz water
100 g/3½ oz plain flour, sifted
2 eggs

Pastry Cream

2 eggs, beaten lightly
4 tbsp caster sugar
2 tbsp cornflour
300 ml/10 fl oz milk
¼ tsp vanilla extract

Icing

2 tbsp butter
1 tbsp milk
1 tbsp cocoa powder
55 g/2 oz icing sugar
white chocolate, broken into pieces

Preheat the oven to 200°C/400°F/Gas Mark 6. Lightly grease a baking tray. Place the water in a saucepan, add the butter and heat gently until the butter melts. Bring to a rolling boil, then remove the saucepan from the heat and add the flour all at once, beating well until the mixture leaves the sides of the saucepan and forms a ball. Leave to cool slightly, then gradually beat in the eggs to form a smooth, glossy mixture. Spoon into a large piping bag fitted with a 1-cm/½-inch plain nozzle.

Sprinkle the baking sheet with a little water. Pipe éclairs 7½ cm/3 inches long, spaced well apart. Bake in the preheated oven for 30–35 minutes, or until crisp and golden. Make a small slit in the side of each éclair to let the steam escape. Leave to cool on a wire rack.

Meanwhile, make the pastry cream. Whisk the eggs and sugar until thick and creamy, then fold in the cornflour. Heat the milk until almost boiling and pour onto the eggs, whisking. Transfer to the saucepan and cook over a low heat, stirring until thick. Remove the saucepan from the heat and stir in the vanilla extract. Cover with baking paper and leave to cool.

To make the icing, melt the butter with the milk in a saucepan, remove from the heat and stir in the cocoa and sugar. Split the éclairs lengthways and pipe in the pastry cream. Spread the icing over the top of the éclairs. Melt a little white chocolate in a heatproof bowl set over a saucepan of gently simmering water, then drizzle over the chocolate icing and leave to set.

pure

indulgence

Black Forest
Gateau

SERVES 8

3 tbsp unsalted butter, melted, plus extra for greasing
900 g/2 lb fresh cherries, stoned and halved
250 g/9 oz caster sugar
100 ml/3½ fl oz cherry brandy
100 g/3½ oz plain flour
50 g/1¾ oz cocoa powder
½ tsp baking powder
4 eggs
1 litre/1¾ pints double cream
grated plain chocolate and whole fresh cherries, to decorate

Preheat the oven to 180°C/350°F/Gas Mark 4. Grease and line a 23-cm/9-inch springform cake pan. Place the cherries in a saucepan, add 3 tablespoons of the sugar and the cherry brandy and bring to a simmer over a medium heat. Simmer for 5 minutes. Sift the flour, cocoa and baking powder together in a large bowl.

Place the eggs in a heatproof bowl and beat in 160 g/5¾ oz of the sugar. Place the bowl over a saucepan of simmering water and beat for 6 minutes, or until thickened. Remove from the heat, then gradually fold in the flour mixture and the melted butter. Spoon into the cake tin and bake for 40 minutes. Remove from the oven and leave to cool in the tin.

Turn out the cake and cut in half horizontally. Mix the cream and the remaining sugar together and whip lightly until soft peaks form. Spread the reserved syrup over the cut sides of the cake, then spread a layer of whipped cream on the bottom half of the cake, followed by the cherries, then place the other half on top. Cover the top of the cake with whipped cream, sprinkle over the grated chocolate and decorate with whole fresh cherries.

Raspberry
Vacherin

SERVES 10

3 egg whites

175 g/6 oz caster sugar

1 tsp cornflour

25 g/1 oz plain chocolate, grated

Filling

175 g/6 oz plain chocolate, plus extra to decorate, broken into pieces

450 ml/16 fl oz double cream, whipped

300 g/10½ oz fresh raspberries

Preheat the oven to 140°C/275°F/Gas Mark 1. Draw 3 rectangles, measuring 10 x 25 cm/4 x 10 inches, on sheets of non-stick baking paper and place on 2 baking trays. Whisk the egg whites in a large, clean bowl until soft peaks form, then gradually whisk in half the sugar and continue whisking until very stiff and glossy. Gently fold in the remaining sugar, the cornflour and grated chocolate with a metal spoon or a palette knife.

Spoon the meringue mixture into a piping bag fitted with a 1-cm/½-inch plain nozzle and pipe lines across the baking paper rectangles. Bake in the preheated oven for 1½ hours, changing the position of the baking trays halfway through. Without opening the oven, turn off the oven and leave the meringues to cool in the oven, then peel off the baking paper. To make the filling, melt the chocolate in a heatproof bowl set over a saucepan of barely simmering water and spread it over 2 of the meringue layers. Leave to set.

Put a chocolate-coated meringue on a plate and top with about one third of the cream and raspberries. Gently put the second chocolate-coated meringue on top and spread with half the remaining cream and raspberries. Put the remaining meringue on top and decorate with the remaining cream and raspberries.

Melt a few extra pieces of plain chocolate in a heatproof bowl set over a saucepan of barely simmering water. Drizzle over the top of the vacherin and serve.

Brownie Base
Cheesecake

MAKES 12

Brownie Base

115 g/4 oz unsalted butter, plus extra for greasing
115 g/4 oz plain chocolate
200 g/7 oz caster sugar
2 eggs, beaten
50 ml /2 fl oz milk
115 g/4 oz plain flour, plus extra for dusting
strawberries dipped in melted plain chocolate, to decorate

Topping

500 g/1 lb 2 oz cream cheese
125 g/4½ oz golden caster sugar
3 eggs, beaten
1 tsp vanilla extract
115 g/4 oz natural yogurt
melted plain chocolate, for drizzling

Preheat the oven to 180°C/350°F/Gas Mark 4. Lightly grease and flour a 23-cm/9-inch square baking tin.

Melt the butter and chocolate in a saucepan over a low heat, stirring until smooth. Remove from the heat and beat in the sugar.

Add the eggs and milk, beating well. Stir in the flour, mixing just until blended. Spoon into the prepared tin, spreading evenly.

Bake in the oven for 25 minutes. Remove from the oven and reduce the oven temperature to 160°C/325°F/Gas Mark 3.

For the topping, beat together the cheese, sugar, eggs and vanilla extract until well blended. Stir in the yogurt, then pour over the brownie base. Bake for a further 45–55 minutes, or until the centre is almost set.

Run a knife around the edge of the cake to loosen from the tin. Let cool before removing from the tin. Chill in the refrigerator for 4 hours or overnight before cutting into slices. Serve drizzled with melted chocolate and with the chocolate-dipped strawberries on the side.

Mocha Layer
Cake

SERVES 8

butter, for greasing
250 g/9 oz self-raising flour
¼ tsp baking powder
4 tbsp cocoa powder
115 g/4 oz caster sugar
2 eggs
2 tbsp golden syrup
150 ml/5 fl oz sunflower oil
150 ml/5 fl oz milk

Filling & Topping

1 tsp instant coffee powder
1 tbsp boiling water
300 ml/10 fl oz double cream
2 tbsp icing sugar

To Decorate

50 g/1¾ oz chocolate shavings
ready-made chocolate caraque
icing sugar, for dusting

Preheat the oven to 180°C/350°F/Gas Mark 4. Lightly grease 3 x 18-cm/7-inch shallow round cake tins.

Sift the flour, baking powder and cocoa powder together into a large bowl. Stir in the caster sugar. Make a well in the centre. Add the eggs, syrup, oil and milk to the well and gradually beat in with a wooden spoon to form a smooth mixture. Divide between the prepared tins. Bake in the preheated oven for 35–45 minutes, or until springy to the touch. Leave to cool slightly in the tins, then transfer to a wire rack and leave to cool completely.

To make the filling, dissolve the coffee in the boiling water and put in a bowl with the cream and icing sugar. Whip until the cream is just holding its shape. Use half the cream to sandwich the 3 cakes together. Spread the remaining cream over the top and sides of the cake. Lightly press the chocolate shavings into the cream around the side of the cake.

Transfer to a serving plate. Lay the chocolate caraque over the top of the cake. Cut a few thin strips of baking paper and arrange on top of the caraque. Dust lightly with icing sugar, then carefully remove the paper.

Chocolate Berry
Dacquoise

SERVES 8

4 egg whites
225 g/8 oz caster sugar
55 g/2 oz ground hazelnuts
225 g/8 oz dark chocolate
350 ml/12 fl oz double cream
2 tbsp kirsch
350 g/12 oz mixed summer berries, such as baby strawberries, raspberries and blueberries

Preheat the oven to 140°C/275°F/Gas Mark 1. Line 3 baking sheets with non-stick baking paper and mark 3 x 18-cm/7-inch rounds on each. Whisk the egg whites until very stiff, then gradually add the sugar, whisking well after each addition. When all the sugar has been added, stir in the ground hazelnuts. Mix lightly until thoroughly incorporated.

Divide the meringue among the 3 baking sheets and then spread evenly within the circles. Bake in the preheated oven for 1–1½ hours, or until the meringues feel firm to the touch. Leave to cool, then remove from the baking sheets. Leave until cold.

Break the chocolate into small pieces, place in a heavy-based saucepan and add 225 ml/8 fl oz of the cream and the kirsch. Heat gently, stirring until melted and smooth. Remove, pour into a bowl, cool, then chill for at least 2 hours, or until set. Once set, whisk until light and fluffy.

Spread two thirds of the chocolate filling over 2 of the meringues and spread to the edges. Arrange most of the fruit over the chocolate filling, reserving the remaining fruit for decoration. Place the meringues one on top of the other, ending with a plain meringue.

Whip the remaining cream until stiff, then reserve a little for decoration and use the remainder to spread round the sides of the meringues. Spread the remaining chocolate on the top meringue and swirl with the tines of a fork. Decorate the top with the remaining berries.

Mississippi
Mud Pie

SERVES 8

Pastry

225 g/8 oz plain flour, plus extra for dusting
2 tbsp cocoa powder
140 g/5 oz butter
2 tbsp caster sugar
1–2 tbsp cold water

Filling

175 g/6 oz butter
350 g/12 oz soft dark brown sugar
4 eggs, lightly beaten
4 tbsp cocoa powder, sifted
150 g/5½ oz plain chocolate
300 ml/10 fl oz single cream
1 tsp chocolate extract

To Decorate

425 ml/15 fl oz double cream, whipped
chocolate flakes
chocolate curls

To make the pastry, sift the flour and cocoa powder into a mixing bowl. Rub in the butter with your fingertips until the mixture resembles fine breadcrumbs. Stir in the sugar and enough cold water to mix to a soft dough. Wrap the dough and chill in the refrigerator for 15 minutes.

Preheat the oven to 190°C/375°F/Gas Mark 5. Roll out the pastry on a lightly floured work surface and use to line a 23-cm/9-inch loose-based flan tin or ceramic flan dish. Line with baking paper and fill with baking beans. Bake in the preheated oven for 15 minutes. Remove the paper and beans from the pastry case and cook for a further 10 minutes until crisp.

To make the filling, beat the butter and sugar together in a bowl and gradually beat in the eggs with the cocoa powder. Melt the chocolate and beat it into the mixture with the single cream and the chocolate extract.

Reduce the oven temperature to 160°C/325°F/Gas Mark 3. Pour the mixture into the pastry case and bake for 45 minutes, or until the filling has set gently.

Let the mud pie cool completely, then transfer the pie to a serving plate, if you like. Cover with the whipped cream. Decorate the pie with chocolate flakes and curls and then chill until ready to serve.

Truffled Honey
Tart

SERVES 6

Pastry

115 g/4 oz plain flour
pinch of salt
75 g/2½ oz cold butter, cut into pieces
1 tsp icing sugar
cold water

Filling

300 g/10½ oz curd cheese
115 g/4 oz cream cheese
125 ml/4 fl oz double cream
2 egg yolks, plus 1 whole egg
2 tbsp caster sugar
4 tbsp flower honey, plus extra for drizzling
crystallized violets or sugared rose petals, to decorate

Lightly grease a 22-cm/9-inch loose-based fluted tart tin. Sift the flour and salt into a food processor, add the butter and process until the mixture resembles fine breadcrumbs. Tip the mixture into a large bowl, add the sugar and a little cold water, just enough to bring the dough together. Turn out onto a work surface dusted with more flour and roll out the pastry to a round 8 cm/3¼ inches larger than the tin. Carefully lift the pastry into the tin and press to fit. Roll the rolling pin over the pan to neaten the edges and trim the excess pastry. Fit a piece of baking paper into the pastry case, fill with baking beans and leave to chill in the refrigerator for 30 minutes. Meanwhile, preheat the oven to 190°C/375°F/Gas Mark 5.

Remove the pastry case from the refrigerator and bake blind for 10 minutes in the preheated oven, then remove the beans and paper and bake for an additional 5 minutes.

Mix the curd cheese, cream cheese and cream together until smooth, then stir in the egg yolks and whole egg with the sugar and honey until completely smooth. Pour into the pastry case and bake for 30 minutes. Remove from the oven and leave to cool in the tin for 10 minutes. Drizzle with more honey and decorate with the violets.

Latticed
Cherry Pie

SERVES 8

Pastry

140 g/5 oz plain flour, plus extra for dusting
¼ tsp baking powder
½ tsp mixed spice
½ tsp salt
50 g/1¾ oz caster sugar
55 g/2 oz cold unsalted butter, diced, plus extra for greasing
1 beaten egg, plus extra for glazing
water, for sealing

Filling

900 g/2 lb stoned fresh cherries, or canned cherries, drained
150 g/5 oz caster sugar
½ tsp almond extract
2 tsp cherry brandy
¼ tsp mixed spice
2 tbsp cornflour
2 tbsp water
25 g/1 oz unsalted butter
freshly whipped cream or ice cream, to serve

Preheat the oven to 220°C/425°F/Gas Mark 7. Grease a 23-cm/9-inch round pie dish with butter. Roll out the pastry into 2 rounds, each 30 cm/12 inches in diameter. Use one to line the pie dish. Trim the edges, leaving an overhang of 1 cm/½ inch. To make the pastry, sift the flour with the baking powder into a large bowl. Stir in the mixed spice, salt and sugar. Using your fingertips, rub in the butter until the mixture resembles fine breadcrumbs, then make a well in the centre. Pour the beaten egg into the well. Mix with a wooden spoon, then shape the mixture into a dough. Cut the dough in half and use your hands to roll each half into a ball. Wrap the dough and chill in the refrigerator for 30 minutes.

To make the filling, put half of the cherries and all of the sugar in a large saucepan. Bring to a simmer over a low heat, stirring, for 5 minutes, or until the sugar has melted. Stir in the almond essence, brandy and mixed spice. In a separate bowl, mix the cornflour and water to form a paste. Remove the saucepan from the heat, stir in the cornflour paste, then return to the heat and stir constantly until the mixture boils and thickens. Leave to cool a little. Stir in the remaining cherries, pour into the pastry case, then dot with butter. Cut the remaining pastry into strips, lay evenly on top of the filling to form a lattice, seal the edges with water, then brush the top with beaten egg to glaze. Cover with foil, then bake for 30 minutes. Remove from the oven, discard the foil, then return the pie to the oven for a further 15 minutes, or until cooked and golden. Serve warm with whipped cream.

almonds
almond & hazelnut cake 23
chocolate fudge cake 10
clementine cake 24
coffee streusel cake 18
fruit & nut squares 54
pecan brownies 41
see also hazelnuts
apples
apple cake 15
upside-down toffee apple brownies 40
apricots
apricot oat-style cookies 51
fruit & nut squares 54

bananas: carrot cake 14
Battenberg cake 16
berries: *see under* individual names
Black Forest gateau 64
blueberries
blueberry bran muffins 59
chocolate berry dacquoise 72

cappuccino brownies 42
carrot cake 14
cheese, cream
carrot cake 14
truffled honey tart 77
cheese, soft: brownie base cheesecake 69
cherries
Black Forest gateau 64
fruit & nut squares 54
latticed cherry pie 78
chocolate
almond & hazelnut cake 23
Black Forest gateau 64
brownie base cheesecake 69
cappuccino brownies 42
chocolate berry dacquoise 72
chocolate chip oaties 46
chocolate éclairs 60
chocolate fudge cake 10
hazelnut chocolate crunch 52
Mississippi mud pie 76
mocha layer cake 70
mocha walnut cookies 50
pecan brownies 41
raspberry vacherin 68
sticky chocolate brownies 36
cinnamon
apple cake 15
drizzled honey cupcakes 28
see also mixed spices
clementine cake 24
see also drizzled honey cupcakes 28
cloves
drizzled honey cupcakes 28
see also mixed spices
cocoa
Battenberg cake 16
Black Forest gateau 64
cappuccino brownies 42
chocolate chip oaties 46
chocolate éclairs 60
chocolate fudge cake 10
Mississippi mud pie 76
mocha layer cake 70
sticky chocolate brownies 36
coffee
cappuccino brownies 42
coffee streusel cake 18
mocha layer cake 70
mocha walnut cookies 50
cooking tips 5
cream, double
almond & hazelnut cake 23
Black Forest gateau 64
chocolate berry dacquoise 72
Mississippi mud pie 76
mocha layer cake 70
raspberry vacherin 68
truffled honey tart 77
cream, single
clementine cake 24
Mississippi mud pie 76
cream, soured: lemon drizzle cake 22
curd cheese: truffled honey tart 77

dried fruit, mixed: rolled fruit buns 58

éclairs, chocolate 60
equipment 5

fruit & nut squares 54
fruits: *see under* individual names

hazelnuts
almond & hazelnut cake 23
chocolate berry dacquoise 72
fruit & nut squares 54
hazelnut chocolate crunch 52
upside-down toffee apple brownies 40
see also almonds; pecan brownies
honey
apple cake 15
apricot oat-style cookies 51
blueberry bran muffins 59
drizzled honey cupcakes 28
fruit & nut squares 54
truffled honey tart 77

latticed cherry pie 78
lavender fairy cakes 34
lemons
lemon butterfly cupcakes 33
lemon drizzle cake 22
moist walnut cupcakes 32
liqueurs
cherry brandy
Black Forest gateau 64
latticed cherry pie 78
Kirsch: chocolate berry dacquoise 72

marzipan: Battenberg cake 16
Mississippi mud pie 76
mixed spices
coffee streusel cake 18
latticed cherry pie 78
rolled fruit buns 58
upside-down toffee apple brownies 40
see also cinnamon; cloves; nutmeg
mocha layer cake 70
mocha walnut cookies 50

nutmeg
drizzled honey cupcakes 28
see also mixed spices
nuts: *see under* individual names

oat bran: blueberry bran muffins 59
oats
apricot oat-style cookies 51
chocolate chip oaties 46
fruit & nut squares 54
hazelnut chocolate crunch 52
oranges
drizzled honey cupcakes 28
see also clementine cake 24

pecan brownies 41
see also hazelnuts
raspberries
chocolate berry dacquoise 72
raspberry vacherin 68

sesame seeds
apricot oat-style cookies 51
fruit & nut squares 54
spices: *see* mixed spices

strawberries
brownie base cheesecake 69
chocolate berry dacquoise 72
syrup
chocolate fudge cake 10
hazelnut chocolate crunch 52
mocha layer cake 70
sticky chocolate brownies 36

truffled honey tart 77

walnuts
carrot cake 14
drizzled honey cupcakes 28
mocha walnut cookies 50
moist walnut cupcakes 32

Victoria sandwich cake 8

yeast: rolled fruit buns 58
yogurt: brownie base cheesecake 69